THE MASONIC TU

C000059588

Making a Master Mason

A Guide to Mastering your Freemasonry

Accept from me the chisel of a liberal education

Making a Master Mason

A Guide to Mastering your Freemasonry

Robert Lomas

For Cliff

Wth Best Wishs

Robert Lomas

DOWAGER BOOKS
WEB OF HIRAM PUBLICATIONS

DOWAGER BOOKS
www.dowager.com

WEB OF HIRAM PUBLICATIONS
www.webofhiram.org

Contents

The Masonic Tutor's Handbooks

The relationship between a Master Mason and the other Brethren of their Lodge is the traditional way that our Craft's traditional wisdom is passed on.

In the fifteenth century, when Freemasonry began, there was no formal education. On-going training took place in working groups (lodges), where the Fellowcrafts and Apprentices worked together with experienced Master Masons to receive continuous guidance, advice and support. The Master Builder would demonstrate and explain the task, and afterwards the Fellowcrafts would implement the worshipful master's ideas whilst being guided and helped towards their own understanding by the Master Masons. The relationship took the form of a legal contract between a Building Master and the Journeyman or Fellowcraft and the Master Masons, who received wages for their work whilst being under the employment of the Building Master. Individuals would begin as Entered Apprentice, who would be taught the skills needed to become a Fellowcraft by an experienced brother. Once they had developed sufficient skill, and proved their understanding of the work, they would eventually become Master Masons, who were entitled to instruct within the lodge and pass on their knowledge of The Craft to the next generation before going on to take on their own building commissions, and employ Apprentices, Craftsmen and Master Masons.

This is how Freemasonry once used to pass on its knowledge and understanding, but in recent times this method has fallen into disuse. There have been attempts to improve 'Masonic Education,' but most of these seem to rely on the provision of online material, and lack the shared personal interaction between Master Masons and their junior brethren. The office of Mentor pays lip service to this tradition, but often becomes just an administrative office, not the intensely personal relationship of a Master Mason working with his junior brethren, which enabled all to learn from each other. This series of books has been written to address this deficit.

Freemasonry is based on Three Grand Principles. Brotherly Love, Relief and Truth.

The Lodge, with its meetings and its social events, illustrates, practices and teaches Brotherly Love.

The Charity Stewards, with their Covenant forms and regular promotional events, show how to carry out the duty of Relief,

But it is down to a Masonic Tutor to demonstrate how to approach and understand Truth.

There are three books in this educational series.

The first, *Vol. 1: The Duties of the Apprentice Master*, was intended to enable a Masonic Tutor to pass on a basic understanding of the content and objectives of the First Degree to a new brother, introduce them to their lodge, and prepare them to be passed to the degree of a Fellowcraft.

The first volume was published before Covid. The second volume, *Freemasonry After Covid*, was published during the first lockdown, when we were forbidden to meet. It contains details of how to use various online methods to help keep the glimmering light in the East alight, during those hard times.

Vol 3: Becoming a Craftsman, the third volume (which is actually the second in the education series) was published as the vaccines started to roll out, and lodges needed to work out how to restart their work and fellowship. It is directed to both the new Fellowcraft and their Tutor, encouraging them to work jointly, to study the hidden mysteries of nature and science together. They are encouraged to study the work of famous Fellowcrafts of the past who excelled in their study of the hidden mysteries and went on to benefit society in general, and the craft in particular.

This third educational book, *Vol 4: Making a Master Mason*, is directed towards a newly raised Master Mason to help that individual learn how the extent of their understanding of the final mystery of the Centre will be the result of their individual effort. The lodge can help develop awareness and deepen understanding by the progression through the offices. But the continuing application of the mental tools the Craft provides to help an individual conceive, design and build their own soul need to be mastered if they desire to progress.

Using this book, Master Masons are encouraged to develop their understanding and teaching skills, to help their lodge thrive by harnessing that urge for knowledge that began in their hearts. Now as Master Masons they are well placed to discover that the knowledge they seek is to be found deep inside themselves.

The chisel symbolizes the process of education and instruction, in the ways of our Ancient Craft. As an Entered Apprentice you were told to make daily steps in Masonic knowledge. To do this you were advised to study the objects of research in each degree. This advice was reinforced in the degree of Fellowcraft, where you were encouraged to study the hidden mysteries of nature and science. Now as Master Mason you are encouraged to develop your perception of The Centre, the point where no Master Mason can materially err, and where the lost secrets of a Master Mason are to be found. You are also encouraged to teach your junior brethren, as, by teaching, you also develop your own understanding.

Education continues to shape your intellect, expand your mind, broaden your perspective, and make you a more civilized human being. The discipline of study, learning and discussion with your brethren, is a good habit to acquire. Master Masons should encourage all Fellowcrafts and Apprentices to make their own daily steps in Masonic knowledge. But the Masonic method of squaring, shaping and polishing your rough ashlar is necessarily slow. The key to success is to develop your own craftsmanship, take pride in your work and appreciate that each stone in the plan of Freemasonry, no matter how apparently oddly shaped, is needed and is vital to complete your structure.

If you think the cost of instruction and education is expensive, consider the immense cost and consequences of ignorance.

Instruction and guidance are how a Master Mason becomes a Masonic Tutor able to explain and demonstrate the philosophical methods of Freemasonry, and to encourage all brethren to develop knowledge and understanding.

This encompasses three areas.

1. Learning how to memorize and deliver ritual.
2. Understanding the duties and lessons of each office in the lodge
3. Applying your understanding of the study of Truth, by learning how to experience the mystery of the Centre.

Introduction

This book is based on my many years' experience of giving lectures and supplying podcasts of Masonic Instruction to new Masons. It is based on the third of a series of lectures I originally created for W. Bro Sandy Macmillan of St Lawrence Lodge in Pudsey, Yorkshire West Riding, to help him teach a group of six newly raised Master Masons understand the Degree they had just been awarded.

Part One contains the content of the lecture I gave them. I used PowerPoint, and there is a set of PowerPoint slides and a script available on the Masonic Tutor Support Website which is offered through the support of the WebofHiram.org which you can use if you wish to present it that way.

It was my experience, however, that when other brethren wanted to deliver this lecture to new Master Masons in their Lodge, they did not always have access to computers, screens, and projectors. So, I created a reading version of the lecture which takes about thirty minutes to deliver and can be read directly from the book. When I deliver the lecture, I always follow it with a question-and-answer session for the new Master Masons, before throwing open the debate to any other brethren. To handle all possible questions requires a wide background knowledge of the degree and its history, and I soon found that, although individuals might be happy to deliver the content, either with slides or by reading, they were not always confident about answering questions. To help them, I set up an online message board, where interesting questions could be posted for me to answer. This Frequently Asked

Question section is to be also available on the Masonic Tutor Support Website, and new questions will be answered for any user of this book who registers for support. It has been my experience that once an individual has given the lecture a few times, either using slides or reading, then they quickly become more confident in answering questions. It is a truism that the best way to learn a subject is to teach it to someone else.

The lecture/reading can be used in several different ways. It can be given during a lodge meeting; it can be given at a lodge of instruction; if there is a group of new Master Masons from different lodges in the same hall, it can be given in a meeting organized just for that group and any interested supporters, or mentors. Each means of delivery works, but there are advantages in bringing together groups of Master Mason in a shared venue, as it will encourage visiting, friendship and discussion.

However, I quickly found there was a need for more support material than just a lecture about the degree. As the purpose of the lecture was to deliver a light-beam of Masonic Enlightenment, I soon realized that breaking up that shaft of light into short sharp items of information helped to reinforce the message. Being a physicist, I naturally called them Photons of Masonic Light, because a photon is the smallest individual component of any light beam. When I first created the Masonic Light programme for Yorkshire West Riding, some fifteen years ago, the phrase nugget came into use, but in some of the rural lodges the term a 'right nugget' had unfortunate overtones. So I prefer to call the little ritual pieces Photons of Masonic Light.

Part Two contains a selection of these Masonic Photons that can be used in various ways. For example, a tutor, mentor, or proposer can deliver a Welcoming Photon directly after the ceremony and before the lodge closes, whilst handing over any mentoring pack or other support material the lodge gives to its new member. Other explanatory Photons can be given during lodges of instruction, or even at Festive Boards. The third degree is the most dramatic and profound of the rituals but can lead to disappointment that no new secrets are delivered. If a newly raised brother is going fully understand the Craft, then they need realise that there is more of the story to be told not yet told.

One important area of Masonic instruction is the formal ritual description of the Tracing Board of the Third Degree and the Traditional History. This can be found in the various ritual books, and if the lodge has a preferred version, then use it. However, these are long and complex pieces to memorize. Just as I found that it was easier for a tutor or proposer to read a set piece of instruction rather than deliver a lecture, so I found a need for a simple reading version of the Third-Degree Tracing Board and The Traditional History, which covers all the landmarks needed to guide the Master Mason's progress.

Part Three contains a simple reading version of The Description of the Third-Degree Tracing Board which can be read directly from the book. (A reading version of the Traditional History can be found in the Photons of Masonic Light Section. When you are reading the Tracing Board is useful to display the lodge's tracing board to the new Master Mason. I would also recommend the creation of a good quality photograph of your lodge's board to give an electronic copy to each Master Mason to put in a hidden folder on their phone to encourage them to study it when they have a quiet moment.

Part Four of this guide offers a way to expand a new Master Mason's awareness of opportunities for personal development the ritual offers by suggesting a way to use all their working tools for self-improvement.

I have spent many years trying to help my fellow masons understand the purpose of the rituals, how the ceremonies are worked, and the objectives of the various degrees. This series of books contains what I have learned and what I hope to impart to help Freemasonry not only survive but thrive as it returns from its long hibernation during the Covid crisis.

I wish you well in that task, Brethren.

Part 1

Polishing Your Perfect Ashlar

Polishing Your Perfect Ashlar

In this section I want to discuss the significance of the Third-Degree secrets. I'm not going to tell you what the secrets are, as they are almost impossible to put into words, but I'm going to tell you how you can set about finding them for yourself, and where you need to look. And let me assure you that all the clues are in the ceremonies and their symbols.

Let's begin by reflecting on how you arrived at your Third Degree. You had already been taught two previous lessons. So, before I discuss the Third Degree, its nature and what it teaches you, let's consider what you already knew.

In the First Degree you were taught how to face your fears. You were blindfolded, and came into the lodge in darkness, while it was in light. You could not see the way forward and you had to be guided. You couldn't see where you were going, so it would have been easy for you to trip over things. This dependency taught you to trust your guides. The Junior Deacon who looked after you had probably guided many previous Candidates on their way.

As a Candidate you learned to practice upright behaviour, to face up to your fears, and to appreciate one of the basic objectives of Freemasonry. There was a moment when you stood before the Master, with a cable-tow about your neck and a hoodwink over your eyes, and the Master said to you. 'What is the predominant wish of your heart?' And what did you reply? You said, 'Light'. As you spoke the assembled brethren gave a loud clap, and your hoodwink was removed. The first thing you saw, as a newly made Entered Apprentice, was the three great lights of our Craft, the square, the compasses and the VSL.

This experience from that first degree means that you know that you must learn to face down your fears, you understand how to control the emotions of your body, and you have discovered how to trust your Masonic guides if you want to progress in Masonic Knowledge.

Now let's reflect on the Second Degree. In that ceremony you learned to study the hidden mysteries of nature and science, how to temper the demands of your emotions with the insight of your intellect. You were advised to look for a spiral stairway which leads you to the throne of the Grand Geometrician, by studying His works. It is that study of the hidden mysteries of nature and science which gives you a clue as to how this world began and if it might have a purpose. You learned how to behave honourably with others and how to balance your emotional responses against your intellectual insights. Most significantly in the Second Degree you entered the lodge in light, as you were no longer hoodwinked. Both you and the lodge worked together in light as you began to investigate the hidden mysteries of nature and science in a joint venture with the brethren of your lodge. You also learned about the inner chamber of the temple, where our ancient brethren went to collect their wages. The junior warden told you, during the closing of the Second Degree, that at the centre of the building you are creating, there is a sacred symbol. It is the same sacred symbol that you see at the centre of the lodge, a G within a flaming star. Now you can be given various versions of what that G might stand for, as traditionally, the symbol is never fully explained to you. It might be Geometry, or the Grand Geometrician of the Universe, or even represent your personal God, but traditionally the symbol is for you to interpret as you wish. You are, however, told that this sacred symbol is at the centre of the building. And you should remember that whenever Freemasonic ritual talks about a building, or the process of building a temple, it is talking about you. It's talking about the way in which you construct your own character, your own personality, your own way of thinking, your soul. The middle chamber of the temple, which is talked about in the Second Degree, where our ancient brethren went to collect their wages is you, it's formed by your character, your personality, your soul. You are that uncompleted temple. And in the Third Degree you learn a lot more about that temple of yourself.

In the Third-degree ceremony you face what's described as your last and greatest trial. This is to confront the concept of your own death. In this degree you enter a darkened lodge room, where the brethren who are accompanying you on this journey are as much in the dark as you are. You have changed from being a poor candidate in a state of darkness entering a lighted lodge, to a degree where both you and the lodge share the darkness of ignorance about its sombre topic. You enter this unknown realm together. But if you are going to learn about Truth you've also got to learn how to overcome your ego, because your ego will try to stop you acknowledging any Truth which threatens its own supremacy.

During this ceremony you need to understand about the symbolic meanings of the directions within the lodge: the North, South, West and East. I am sure you recall that you first met them in the First-Degree tracing board. In this degree their import becomes clearer. The description of Solomon's Temple in some volumes of the sacred law says that it only had one gate. And yet the temple you explore in the darkened lodge room has three gates, each facing in a different direction and each guarded by a different sort of ruffian who wants to attack you.

Let's spend a little time thinking about these symbolic directions so you have them firmly fixed in your mind before we start to consider what the degree is trying to teach you.

Bro Walter Leslie Wilmshurst, founder of the Lodge of Living Stones, created a Tracing Board of the Centre which he used to teach the nature of these directions. It has the East, the West, and an implied North and South. In the centre of this diagram there is a circle. This circle symbolises a Mason standing in the centre of their lodge. The Mason is symbolically made up of four parts, each the fourth part of the circle. As Brother Junior Warden frequently reminds us, during the opening and closing of a Fellowcraft lodge, a square is an angle of 90 degrees, or the fourth part of circle.

Each of these square segments represents a different characteristic of a Mason. Wilmshurst suggests thinking of them as the Aristotelian elements, Earth, Water, Air and Fire. They symbolise your fearful emotions, your intellect, your ego, and your spirit. Until you can bring these four parts of your nature into balance you are not going to achieve awareness of the Centre. Only when you learn how to balance the three conflicting parts of your personality is your spirit free to perceive the centre. The circle which represents your inner conflict is placed within the lodge and the directions in the lodge also have an influence on you. Each direction has a meaning. The North is the side of ignorance and unenlightenment. It represents the condition of the novice whose spiritual latent awareness has not yet risen within his consciousness. That is where you sit when you first join the lodge, in the darkness of the North.

The South, where Brother Junior Warden sits, is where the sun stands at its meridian at high twelve, and in the latitudes of Jerusalem where Solomon's Temple was built, at some seasons when the sun is at high twelve you cast no shadow. The South denotes knowledge and intellectual light at its zenith. The Junior Warden is the officer who calls us from labour to refreshment, and from refreshment to labour, that profit and pleasure may be the mutual result.

The South represents knowledge, and the North represents ignorance. But you don't want to become an insufferable a know-it-all by moving too far to the South, so that you think you know absolutely everything and have nothing to learn. Neither do you want to stay in the dark, fearful, ignorance of the North. You need to find a point of balance between the two extremes and that moves you to the Centre.

Now let's think about the West. In the West sits the Senior Warden who represents the rational mind of the lodge. Bro Senior Warden is the officer who must make sure that the hireling is paid, and all the brethren are satisfied. This duty is acknowledged and confirmed to have been completed, as the lodge is closed.

Brother Senior Warden represents common sense, the rational mind of the lodge, if you like. The Senior Warden is the logical, scientific, principle in the lodge, the part that keeps things working. The West symbolises rational, materialistic, common sense where the hireling is paid, and all the brethren are satisfied. The Senior Warden's job is to ensure the smooth running of the lodge but what about the East?

As the sun rises in the East to open and enliven the day so is the worshipful master placed in the East to open the lodge to employ, and instruct, their brethren in Freemasonry. The worshipful master sits in the light of the sunrise. The office of worshipful master represents the Light in East, also known as Spirituality, the highest and most sacred mode of consciousness that you can experience. It symbolises your spirit, the flame that the ceremony is trying to ignite within a newly raised master mason. The flame of the spirit, symbolised by the upward pointing square, or fire triangle, is personified in the worshipful master. Even during the darkness of the Third Degree the Master's flame never goes out. But as you move to the centre of the lodge, symbolising your own centre, another pair of conflicting forces pull at you. You've got the tug of rational materialism from the West, represented by the Senior Warden, and the pull of religious fervour luring you towards the East. But again, just as you don't want to become too much of an anally retentive accountant in the West, neither do you want to become a religious fanatic at the East. Once again you should seek a point of balance and that point of balance is found at the centre. The directions of lodge represent the conflicting forces that you will feel within society, the forces of ignorance, the forces of knowledge, the forces of rationality and the forces of mystical spirituality. They are all tugging at you and if you pull too far in any direction you will end up out of balance. You need to find the point of equilibrium, and that is at the centre. But just as you must balance the four parts of your internal circle, you also have to balance your place within the lodge and within society. The first two degrees taught you about balancing your emotions and your intellect, how to adjust your position between the bliss of ignorance and the harsh reality of knowledge. Now, in the Third degree you learn how to balance your balance between irrational spiritual fervour and depressing materialism. Hopefully these steps in Masonic knowledge will show you that you need to work to find that centre but as you seek it what will happen to the conflicting forces within you?

This is where the symbolism of gates helps your understanding. In the Third Degree your three inner parts that need to come into balance, to free the fire of your spirit, are symbolised by three gates, the Gate of Will in the North, the Gate of Intellect in the South, and the Gate of Spiritual Feelings in the East. Remember that when Freemasonry talks of a building it is talking about you. The uncompleted temple is your character, personality, spirit, and soul. There are three gates to your centre, to that Divine Spark which is the centre of your being.

You can try to approach the Centre via the Gate of Will, the Gate of Intellect, or the Gate of Spiritual Feeling. But none of them are going to take you directly to the answer to that key question, what is Truth? At each gate there stands a ruffian, a part of you that wants to challenge the secret that this degree is trying to impart to you. Until you face down these ruffians you will not understand yourself. This final trial teaches you about yourself. The lesson starts at high twelve, when you cast no shadow, when the sun is at its meridian, and you are placed in the centre of your own uncompleted temple. But three forces, symbolised by three ruffians, each try to destabilise you.

You meet the first ruffian at the South Gate, (portrayed by the Junior Warden) when you try to escape out Truth through the Gate of Intellect and Knowledge. You think that you can reason your way out of this dilemma. Perhaps by talking to the Junior Warden you can reason your way out of this. So, your intellect, afraid of having to trust its feelings, afraid of having to confront deep purposes, afraid even to consider its own death faces the Junior Warden. This officer represents the knowledge stored in your intellect, symbolising that part of yourself that does not want to confront its own limitations, then demands the secret of the Centre from you. It refuses to let your spirit rise free and instead strikes you down with a plumb rule. You are so shaken that you go down on one knee, but you don't give in to it. You don't give away the Truth that is hidden within you to that ruffian at the South Gate.

Instead, you stagger to the North Gate, the Gate of Will. You try to argue that if you practice charity and good works you don't need to do anything else. That idea is symbolised by the part of your lower self that doesn't want to reform its bad habits, that doesn't want to curb its excesses. As you reach the North Gate you realised the brute calculation did not work. The Junior Warden struck you down. Perhaps by talking to the Senior Warden you can bribe your way out of this by proclaiming your good works of Charity. So, afraid of having to trust your selfish feelings, afraid of having to confront deep purposes, afraid even to consider you own death you face the Senior Warden, who represents your deep motives. The Senior Warden, portraying that part of yourself that does not want to confront its own limitations, demands the Truth of the Centre from you. Again, you refuse. So, the Senior Warden strikes you down using a Level, the symbol of equality. You are so shocked by this reversal that in your confused and weakened state you throw yourself on the mercy of religious fervour and stagger towards the East Gate.

At this Gate of Spiritual Feeling, you give yourself up to the extremes of religious fanaticism, you throw yourself on the mercy of the Master in the East, but still refuse to reveal the Truth of the Centre. The Worshipful Master strikes you dead with a heavy maul. You have now learned that you cannot reason your way out, you cannot bluster your way out, and you cannot pray your way out. Death is inevitable. It cannot be reasoned away, bought off by charity, or prayed away. This is the low point of the ceremony where you are forced to accept the reality of your own death.

You are now laid in your grave. You are forced to lie still and reflect while the brethren process round you in the flickering darkness and force you to listen to your own funeral music. We all wonder at that low point if life is meaningless. Is there any purpose to it? Is it all a meaningless muddle? Does everything we try to do fail, and in the end, we simply die? But that is not the message of this degree. As you lie there dead and despairing, the real purpose of the degree finally starts to become clear. That meaning is symbolised by the rising of the Bright Morning Star.

As you lie in your grave you are approached by the principal officers of the lodge, to reinforce the previous lessons of each degree. The Junior Warden tries to lift you with the emotional grip of an Entered Apprentice, but it fails. The light of the South is not sufficient to raise you, it proves a slip. Then the Senior Warden comes from the West to try and lift you from your grave using the grip of an intellectual Fellowcraft, but it likewise proves a slip. You still cannot return to the companions of your former toil. Only the Master gives you any hope of being saved. Your only hope lies in that faint glimmer of light in the East. The Master does succeed in raising you, on the five points of fellowship, using the Lion's grip at which point the Bright Morning Star rises on the Eastern horizon.

It is worth reprising briefly what you have learned about light and the rising of the sun in the previous degrees. When you came into the lodge as a Candidate, about to become an Entered Apprentice, you were placed in the North-East Corner of the lodge on the line of the sunrise on the day of greatest light. Because you came into the lodge seeking light, to symbolise that predominant wish you were placed on the line of the sunrise on the day of the summer solstice. When you became a Craftsman, you were moved to the South-East Corner, where the sun rises on the day of greatest darkness. This was to symbolise that you were soon to face the great trial of the Valley of Death. You were forced to confront the great question, what is the purpose of Life? Is it just to fiddle about, get things wrong, and die? That is where you were first symbolically warned about the despair of darkness as you learned to face up to Truth as a Fellowcraft. But if you were internalising the lessons of balance, you were discovering how to evaluate and respond to the forces within society, represented by the directions within the lodge, and how to resolve the conflicts within your own nature. The Craft will help you discover that there is a point of balance of all these forces, and it is at the centre of the Temple, at your own centre.

When the Master raises you with the Lion's Grip on the five points of Fellowship, you are aligned on the East-West line. That symbolises the vernal equinox, when day and night are in perfect equilibrium, when light and dark are perfectly balanced. You are raised on the sunrise line of balanced light and dark.

You came into Freemasonry seeking light and were placed on the sunrise line of the day of greatest light. As a Fellowcraft you faced up to the trials of understanding Truth on the sunrise line of the day of least light. But you were raised on the sunrise line of the day of perfect balance. You are raised on the five points of fellowship and when the Master takes your arm and turns you to look at the emblems of mortality illuminated by the light of the Bright Morning Star you are assured that your life does have purpose.

To understand your purpose there are two further things you need to know. How you set about discovering your purpose, and where you need to look to find it.

The ceremony has shown you that without the support of your brethren it is not easy to discover the Truth. The lodge is greater than any individual member and it encompasses many roles. You have learnt that Freemasonry is progressive. And it is that progression which helps you gain insight.

When you first knocked on the door of the lodge, you were a passive Candidate. You then went through the three degrees and had Freemasonry done to you. Then, as you become an active officer of the lodge and progressed from Inner Guard through to Master. At each stage you did Freemasonry to other people, but in each office, you did different aspects of Masonry, learning something new from each. Eventually you will be the one who strikes the fatal blow, and then raises that individual brother to knowledge of the point of balance at the centre. Each time you carry out an office you learn something more about the ceremony that you are a part of. You don't learn much as you go through as a Candidate, you learn more when you do it other people, but you won't fully understand Truth until you reach the reflective office of the Immediate Past Master. Then you can sit silent, and watch people doing Freemasonry to others and start to understand what it all means. Once you have reflected on life and its purpose, and become aware of the Centre, you are ready to teach the next generation.

So where do you look for that Truth? How do you refine yourself from the rough ashlar, freshly wrenched from the quarry to the smooth ashlar which is perfectly polished and fit to take its place in the yet to be completed temple of your humanity? You have got to create a perfect ashlar, a perfectly squared block, by using your mental tools on yourself.

You have consistently been told in all the degrees that Truth lies within you. If you can bring yourself into balance, then you will move to your centre. You are told about the centre in the climax of the ceremony of the third degree, just after you have been raised, when the Master turns you to look at the open grave and shows you the emblems of mortality. They symbolise that within your mortal frame resides a Divine Spark which gives you purpose. They explain that you are a part of the creating force of the whole Cosmos and must look for purpose within yourself. It's up to you to discover exactly what that means in your life. It's only when you have gone through all the degrees and all the offices that you start to understand. The degree of Immediate Past Master is where things begin to make sense.

So let me sum up the Third Degree. The final secrets that you were given are:

First, remember that you are going to die. So, get on with what you have to do. Don't procrastinate, don't put things off, do it while you can.

Second, listen to your inner vital and immortal principle that understands the Cosmos. If you sit quietly and concentrate on reaching that spark within yourself, it will reveal its secrets to you, so you will learn what Truth is, and what you should do.

And finally, lift your eyes to the bright morning star rising in the East and let it bring peace and tranquillity to you and the faithful and obedient of the human race. You are then fit to take your place in your lodge as a balanced individual, and also help to balance society. In this way Freemasonry gives you the chance to discover a purpose for your life and to explain how you should set about understanding that purpose, whilst teaching you how to work with others to achieve it.

Bro Wilmshurst's created a Tracing Board of the Centre that sums up the entire purpose of the Craft. It shows the Bright Morning Star rising in the East, and the perfect circle of the Master Mason split into his four component square segments, coming in as a Candidate blind and seeking the light of the Apprentice. Then as a Craftsman seeking to study the hidden mysteries of nature and science before moving on to become a Master Mason, becoming balanced and learning how to control the ego, and eventually freeing the fire of the spirit to understand that the centre is that point from which your soul cannot materially err.

As an Initiate your shadow was cast from the rising point of the sun on the day of greatest light (NE), as you went into the second degree your shadow was cast from the sunrise on the shortest day (SE). When you were raised on the five points of fellowship your shadow fell straight from the East to the West. And as the fire of your spirit is freed, you stand at the balance point at the centre of the lodge, with the harmony of the lodge supporting you.

At the central point, from which no Mason can ever err, you cast no stain of a shadow. You have become a Master Mason.

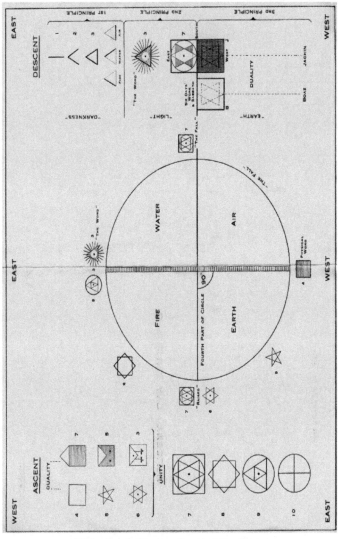

Wilmshurst's Tracing Board of the Centre

Part 2

Photons of Masonic Enlightenment

Photons of Masonic Enlightenment

A photon is the smallest individual particle of light. This section contains some short pieces that address separate points of interest to a new Master Mason, each one adding an individual particle to the flow of Masonic Enlightenment. The sum of a stream of photons creates a beam of the Light of Masonic Truth.

The photons can be used by mentors and tutors to celebrate a new degree, or to answer questions that arise. They can be given during practice nights, or at lodges of instruction. They can even be incorporated into a response from a visitor who has just attended a ceremony, and the advice and insight they contain shared with the new brother to help them feel welcomed and valued.

OVERVIEW OF THE THREE DEGREES OF THE CRAFT

Now you have completed all of the Craft Degrees, it might be useful to summarize what you have been taught so far.

The First degree taught you to face up to your fears, to trust your brethren and offered you the possibility to better know yourself.

In the Tracing Board of the First Degree, you were shown the ground floor of the Temple that you are now building. That Temple represents your own character, and the Board shows the starting point to be a rough ashlar in the North-East corner of the Lodge. On the chequered ground floor of your building three pillars are set, which stand below the canopy of the heavens. These represent the pillars of the Craft. Wisdom, Strength and Beauty. You might also interpret them as Brotherly

Love, Relief and Truth. If you have Wisdom, you share Brotherly Love, if you have Strength, you can provide the Relief of charity to the needy and if you can recognise Truth, you can appreciate its inherent Beauty.

You will also notice many tools and furniture on the floor of this building site. These are to use for the construction of the ground floor of your personal temple. As symbols work on your emotions, not through logic, you will need to think about the symbolism of the tracing board so that it can begin to work its magic on transforming your personality for the better.

The Second degree encouraged you to develop your intellect by studying the mechanisms of nature. This work teaches you to face up to all aspects of Truth and hints that there is a sacred symbol hidden in the centre of the temple of your character that you are building.

You were offered a Tracing Board to show you how to build a second story to this Temple of yourself. Having developed your emotional understanding on the ground floor, you are now encouraged to build a second level, approached by the winding staircase, to develop your intellect.

In the middle chamber of this second floor, you will be paid the wages you have earned, but first you must demonstrate to the wardens who guard it that you are worthy to receive them. You are told in the ritual, as well as in the symbolism of the tracing board, that there is a sacred mystery at the centre of your Temple which you can only reach by ascending to a higher level of understanding.

The Third degree reminded you that you are mortal, that human life is finite and that you must use it well. It showed you that although your ego could easily become the victim of assault by the more aggressive aspects of your nature, if you face up to these attacks, the Divine

Spark within your Centre can be freed to enlighten your character.

You learned of the need to suppress your ego and accept your mortality, so that you can finally see the light of knowledge rising in the East.

As light streams in through the dormer of the upper story of your personal temple, so will it inspire you to realise that the sacred symbol of the Divine spark is not only within the centre of your self-built temple but is also at the centre of your soul.

This Tracing Board emphasises mortality with the symbol of the grave, but the grave is more than a disposal pit; it is marked by a symbol of hope, the Sprig of Acacia.

Around it are strewn tools of planning and measurement – the pencil, skirrit and compasses, along with a plan, which you must now create by using the tools to shape your character.

This board helps you understand that even though you are mortal, and your body must die, your thoughts, plans and aspirations can live on and help you uncover the real import of the Divine spark at your centre.

Our Craft story ends here; however, it leaves at least two anomalies, which might already be in your mind.

The first is: Who exactly is Hiram Abif? The ritual tells you: 'as you are doubtless already aware, he was the principal architect [of King Solomon's Temple].'

Were you aware? Where in the ritual did you become aware? You probably didn't -- because unless you were guided through all the many sections of the Catechismal lectures that knowledge is not imparted.

The second is: In the opening of the Third you heard that the 'genuine secrets of a Master Mason had been lost, but that the Lodge would help you find them.

But ritual didn't deliver. All it could offer were some substituted secrets! Why? If three knew the 'genuine secrets' but only one died, then those secrets must still exist somewhere!

The great teaching myth of Freemasonry is fragmented but not lost. Brethren.

KEEP SEARCHING!

WHY HAVE THIRD DEGREE TEST QUESTIONS?

At the conclusion of your Raising, you were told there are a series of Test Questions and Answers to learn as part of this degree.

Let me first remind you of what they are.

Q1: How were you prepared to be raised to the Third Degree?

A1: By having both arms, both breasts and both knees made bare, and both heels slipshod.

Q2: On what were you admitted?

A2: On both points of the compasses being presented to my naked breasts.

Q3: On your entrance into the Lodge did you observe anything different in this Degree?

A3: I did. All was dark save a glimmering light in the East.

Q4: To what does that darkness allude?

A4: To the darkness of death.

Q5: Is death, then, the peculiar object of research in this Degree?

A5: It is indeed.

Q6: From what circumstances?

A6: From the untimely death of our Grand Master, Hiram Abif.

Q7: What were the instruments used at his destruction?

A7: The Plumb Rule, the Level, and the heavy Setting Maul.

Q8: How became you acquainted with these circumstances?

A8: By having figuratively represented him at the time I was raised to the sublime degree of a Master Mason.

Q9: How were you raised?

A9: On the five points of Fellowship.

Q10: Which I will thank you to name, and briefly explain.

A10: Hand to hand, foot to foot, knee to knee, breast to breast, and hand over back

Hand to hand, I greet you as a Brother.

Foot to foot, that my feet shall traverse through dangers and difficulties, to unite with his in forming a column of mutual defence and support.

Knee to knee, that the posture of my daily supplication to the Most High shall remind me of his wants.

Breast to breast, that my breast shall be the safe and sacred repository of all his true and lawful secrets, when given to me as such.

Hand over back, that I will defend and support a Master Mason's character in his absence, as though he were present.

In the two previous degrees you had to learn a set of test questions as a test of merit to be allowed to enter a superior degree. Think hard about why you have been asked to learn these questions if the degree of Master Mason seems to be a disappointing end to your journey?

WHAT IS THE CENTRE?

The Centre is a vital concept in the Third Degree, as during the opening of a Master Mason's Lodge the WM says, 'I now declare this Master Mason's Lodge duly and properly opened on the Centre, and that for the purpose of Masonry in the Third Degree.'

But what is the Centre that the lodge is opened upon?

During the opening ritual a definition is given of the Centre. Let me just remind you of this sequence.

The Master first asks the JW, 'Whence come you?' The JW replies, 'From the East.' The Master then asks the SW, 'Whither directing your steps?' The SW replies, 'Towards the West.'

The Master then asks the JW, 'Why leave the East and go to the West?' and receives the reply, 'In search of that which was lost.' The Master then asks the SW 'What was it which was lost?' The SW replies 'The genuine secrets of a Master Mason.'

Returning to the JW the Master asks 'How became they lost?' And the JW replies 'By the untimely death of our Grand Master Hiram Abif.' The Master next asks the SW 'How do you hope to find them?' and receives the reply, 'At the Centre.'

Having established the importance of the Centre as the repository of the true secrets of a Master Mason, the ritual then provides a symbolic definition of the Centre.

The Master asks the JW, 'What is a Centre?' The JW replies, 'That point, within a circle from which every part of its circumference is equidistant.' The Master next asks the SW 'And why at the Centre?' to receive the reply 'Because that is the point from which no Master Mason can materially err.'

So, the ritual tells you the purpose of a Master Mason's lodge is to develop an awareness of the Centre to discover the real secrets of Freemasonry. What those secrets are and how you can discover them is left for you to decide.

To help you in this quest let's look at the words of Masonic writer Walter Wilmshurst. He investigated the deeper meaning of this ritual of the Centre in his book *The Meaning of Masonry*. What is the Centre? Is a question that goes right to Wilmshurst's intentions when founding The Lodge of Living Stones, which was to study and teach about the mystery of the Centre.

He was fascinated by a phenomenon that he called 'Cosmic Consciousness' which he was convinced lay at the Centre of Masonic ritual gave it a deep, and often hidden purpose, which underlies the practice of Freemasonry.

At the consecration of The Lodge of Living Stones, Wilmshurst's words made clear that his intention in founding it was to create a 'Centre of Spiritual Energy' to facilitate a channel for a flow of psychic energy between what he called the Heaven-worlds and the lodge on Earth.

Let me now move onto how Wilmshurst further explained these ideas during his address as founding master.

> This Lodge has been formed to meet a demand that is increasingly heard in the Craft, for a fuller understanding and realisation of the latent teachings of our Order. The purpose and the work of any new Lodge must fall within the purview of the three great foundation-principles of the Masonic Order, Brotherhood, Relief, Truth. I wish to stress that hitherto, the energies of the Craft have been directed to the promotion of the first two, to the neglect of the third. The pressure of existence and the conditions of social, intellectual, and religious life are forcing thoughtful minds to a more earnest and intensive search for Truth than ever before. By Truth I mean, not the mere personal virtue of truthfulness, nor even the sectional

truths which sciences, philosophies, churches, and other educative departments of ordinary culture inculcate, but rather that larger Verity which lies behind, comprehends, and finally explains, all these secrets of our Craft, which are worth the finding. They are incommunicable and must be personally experienced within the consciousness of every seeker who is in earnest to translate our ritual and symbolical representations into facts of personal spiritual experience. By squaring the centre, your spirit can uncover its own divine purpose, as the expression of a deep and abiding reality encompassing the ultimate mystery of the centre and the crown of all things.

Many brethren think of the Craft as just a 'system of morality,' and overlook its system of self-knowledge, for which morality is but preparative. A secret Order, with solemn dedicatory prayers, obligations of secrecy, and references to the attainment of a higher than earthly wisdom is not needed to teach morality. But it is to promote a sacred, secret science dealing with the mysteries of being and the quest for Reality that we call 'the Centre.'

Wilmshurst had a clear perception that there is a mystery at the centre of Freemasonry which he recognised as way to create a channel for spiritual energy and insight from what he called The Centre. But did he offer any further insight into what he meant by that term? I think he did.

In March 1924, he wrote an article entitled *Notes on Cosmic Consciousness* where he described a mental phenomenon, which he believed was a means to open a channel to create a flow of spiritual energy between 'the Heaven-worlds and the Lodge on Earth'.

He described what an individual experienced during this phenomenon.

Feeling he was wrapped around by a flame-coloured cloud of light that came from within himself. Directly afterwards he felt a sense of exultation, of immense joyousness accompanied, by an intellectual illumination impossible to describe. Into his brain streamed a momentary lightning-flash of the Brahmic Splendour which has ever since lightened his life; upon his heart fell one drop of Brahmic Bliss, leaving thenceforward for always an aftertaste of heaven. He saw and knew that the Cosmos is not dead matter but a living Presence, that the soul is immortal, that the universe is so built and ordered that without any peradventure all things work together for the good of each and all, that the foundation principle of the world is what we call love, and that the happiness of everyone is in the long run absolutely certain. He learned more within the few seconds during which the illumination lasted than in previous years of study, and he learned much that no study could ever have taught.

For Wilmshurst, awareness of the Centre is a chance for each Master Mason to undergo a personal encounter with the Great Architect. He founded his Lodge of Living Stones to study how this might be taught.

Wilmshurst was not the only writer to speak of this experience. Albert Einstein had also described this same phenomenon in a 1930 article. This is what he said.

Common to all religions is the anthropomorphic character of their conception of God. In general, only individuals of exceptional endowments, and exceptionally high-minded communities, rise to any considerable extent above this level. But there is a third stage of religious experience which belongs to all of them, even though it is rarely found in a pure form: I shall call it cosmic religious feeling. It is very difficult to elucidate this feeling to anyone who is entirely without it, especially as there is no anthropomorphic conception of God corresponding to it.

The individual feels the futility of human desire and aims and the sublimity and marvellous order which reveal themselves both in nature and the world of thought. Individual existence impresses him as a sort of prison, and he wants to experience the universe as a single significant whole.

Wilmshurst's awareness of the Centre is a personal form of that 'cosmic religious feeling' that Einstein describes. During this 'God Experience' the subjects feel themselves unite with all space-time. People who undergo these incidents describe them as either spiritually mystical states or peak experiences.

Wilmshurst created a structured approach to achieving this state of Cosmic Consciousness that he believed was to be found at the Centre. He did it by a process of active meditation, facilitated by thoughtful working of Masonic Rituals. He gave the Lodge of Living Stones a progression to take a Candidate from the door of the lodge to the chair of IPM, with each step bringing that individual a step closer to knowledge of the Centre, the point at which no Mason can materially err.

Wilmshurst's pattern was laid out in his "*Book of the Perfect Lodge*" and shows a path through the offices of the lodge to reach the Centre. It is also symbolically illustrated in his Tracing Board of the Centre, which can be found at the end of the this section.

Let me leave this subject with one final thought. The implication of the ritual is that the circumference of our lodge is infinite. The study of geometry tells us that the centre of an infinite circle must be an infinite array of points, which consequently implies that The Centre is to be found everywhere, and especially within yourself.

The quest Walter Wilmshurst bequeathed to all Master Masons, is to learn how to access the wisdom of that Cosmic Consciousness that is to found within your own Centre.

THE TRADITIONAL HISTORY OF THE THIRD DEGREE

Having taken the great and solemn Obligation of a Master Mason, you have now a right to demand that last and greatest trial, by which alone you can be admitted to a participation of the Secrets of the Third Degree. But first let me call your attention to a retrospect of those Degrees through which you have already passed, by which you will be the better enabled to distinguish and appreciate the connection of our whole system, and the relative dependency of its several parts.

Your admission among Masons, in a state of helpless indigence, was an emblematical representation of the entrance of all men on this their mortal existence; it inculcated the useful lessons of natural equality and mutual dependence; it instructed you too, in the active principles of universal beneficence and charity, and to seek the solace of your own distress by extending relief and consolation to your fellow-creatures in the hour of their affliction. But, above all, it taught you to bend with humility and resignation to the will of the Great Architect of the Universe, and to dedicate your heart, thus purified from every baneful and malignant passion, and fitted only for the reception of truth and wisdom, as well as to His glory and the welfare of your fellow-creatures.

Proceeding onwards, and still guiding your steps by the principles of moral truth, you were led, in the Second Degree, to contemplate the intellectual faculties, and to trace them in their development through the paths of heavenly science, even to the throne of God Himself. The secrets of nature and the principles of intellectual truth were then unveiled to your view.

To your mind, thus modelled by virtue and science, nature, however, presents one great and useful lesson more: she prepares you by contemplation for the closing hour of your existence, and, when by means of that contemplation she has conducted you through the intricate windings of this mortal state, she finally instructs you how to die.

Such, my Brother, is the peculiar object of this, the Third Degree of Freemasonry; it invites you to reflect on this awful subject, and teaches you to feel that, to the just and virtuous individual, death has no terrors equal to the stain of falsehood and dishonour. Of this great truth the annals of Masonry afford us a glorious example in the unshaken fidelity and noble death of our Grand Master, Hiram Abif, who was slain just before the completion of King Solomon's Temple, at the construction of which he was, as you have already been informed, the principal architect. The manner of his death was as follows:

Fifteen Fellowcrafts of that superior class of workmen who were appointed to preside over the rest, seeing that the Temple was nearly finished, and that they were not in possession of the Secrets of the Third Degree, conspired together to obtain them by any means, and even to have recourse to violence, On the eve however, of carrying their scheme into execution, twelve of them recanted; but three, of a more determined and atrocious character than the others, still persisted in their impious design, in prosecution of which they planted themselves respectively at the East, North and South doors of the Temple, whither our Master had retired to pay his adoration to the Most High, as was his wonted custom at the hour of high twelve. His devotions being ended he attempted to return by the South door, where he was accosted by the first of those ruffians, who, for want of other weapons, had armed himself with a heavy Plumb-rule, and in a threatening manner demanded of him the Secrets of a Master Mason, warning him that death would be the consequence of a refusal. Our Master, however, true to his Obligation, answered that those Secrets were known but to three in the world – Solomon, King of Israel; Hiram, King of Tyre; and himself – and that without the consent and co-operation of the other two, he neither could nor would divulge them, but intimated he had no doubt that diligence and patience would in time entitle the worthy Mason to a participation in them; but, for himself, he would rather suffer death than betray the sacred trust reposed in him. This answer not proving satisfactory, the ruffian aimed a violent blow at the head of our Master, but, being startled by the firmness of his demeanour, it missed his forehead, but glanced with such force on his right temple as to cause him to reel and sink on his left knee.

Recovering from this shock, our Master made for the North where he was opposed by the second ruffian who he answered as in the former instance, but with undiminished firmness, when the villain, who was armed with a heavy Level, struck him a violent blow on the left temple, which brought him to the ground on his right knee. Our Master, now finding all chance of escape cut off at both those quarters, staggered, faint and bleeding, to the East door, where the third ruffian was posted, who, on receiving a similar reply to his insolent demand (for even at this trying moment our Master remained firm and unshaken), and being armed with a heavy setting-maul, struck him a violent blow on the forehead, which laid him lifeless at his feet.

Remember now thy Creator in the days of thy youth, while the evil days come not, nor the years draw nigh, when thou shalt say, I have no pleasure in them; While the sun, or the light, or the moon or the stars, be not darkened, nor the clouds return after the rain: In the day when the keepers of the house shall tremble, and the strong men shall bow themselves, and the grinders cease because they are few, and those that look out of the windows be darkened. And the doors shall be shut in the streets, when the sound of the grinding is low, and shall rise up at the voice of the bird, and all the daughters of music shall be brought low; Also when they shall be afraid of that which is high, and fears shall be in the way, and the almond tree shall flourish, and the grasshopper shall be a burden, and desire shall fail: because man goeth to his long home and the mourners go about the streets: Or even the silver cord be loosed, or the golden bowl be broken, or the pitcher be broken at the fountain, or the wheel broken at the cistern. Then shall the dust return to the earth as it was: and the spirit shall return unto God who gave it.

Let me now beg you to observe that the light of a Master Mason is but darkness visible, serving only to express that gloom which rests on the prospect of futurity; it is that mysterious veil of darkness which the eye of human reason cannot penetrate, unless assisted by that light which is from above; yet, even by this glimmering ray you may perceive that you now stand on the very brink of that grave into which you have just figuratively descended, and which, when a few short years shall have passed away, will again receive you into its cold bosom. Let the emblems of mortality which now lie around you, lead you to contemplate your inevitable destiny, and guide your reflections into that most interesting of all human studies, the knowledge of yourself. Be careful to perform thine allocated task while it is day, for the night soon cometh when no man can work. Continue to listen to the voice of nature, which bears witness that even in this perishable frame resides a vital an immortal principle, inspiring a holy confidence that the Lord of Life will enable us to trample the king of terrors beneath our feet and lift our eyes to that bright Morning Star whose rising brings peace and salvation to the faithful and obedient of the human race.

It is thus, my Brother, that all Master Masons are raised from a figurative death to a reunion with companions of their former toils. You, my Brother, have represented one of the brightest characters recorded in the annals of Masonry, namely, our Grand Master, Hiram Abif who lost his life in consequence of his unshaken fidelity to the trust reposed in him. And this, I hope, will make a lasting impression your mind, should you ever be placed in a similar state of trial.

The loss so important as that of the principal architect could not fail to be generally and severely felt; the want of those plans and designs, which had hitherto been so regularly supplied to the different classes of workmen, being the first indication that some heavy calamity had befallen our Master. The Menatschm, or Prefects, or more familiarly speaking, Overseers, deputed some of the most eminent of their number to acquaint King Solomon with the utter confusion into which the absence of Hiram had plunged them, and to express their apprehension that to some fatal catastrophe must be attributed his sudden and mysterious disappearance. King Solomon immediately ordered a general muster of the workmen throughout the different departments, when three of the same class of Overseers were not to be found. On the same day the twelve craftsmen who had originally joined in the conspiracy came before the King and made a voluntary confession of all they knew concerning it, down to the time of withdrawing themselves from the number of the conspirators. This naturally increased the fears of King Solomon for the safety of his chief artist; and he accordingly selected fifteen trusty Fellowcrafts and ordered them to make diligent search after the person of our Master, if he were yet alive, or had suffered death in the attempt to extort from him the Secrets of his exalted Degree. Accordingly, a stated day having been appointed for their return to Jerusalem, they formed themselves into three Fellowcraft Lodges, and departed from the three entrances of the Temple. Many days were spent in fruitless search; indeed, one Lodge returned to Jerusalem without having made any discovery of importance, but a second Lodge was more fortunate, for on the evening of a certain day, after having suffered the greatest privation and personal fatigue, one of the Brethren who had rested himself in a reclining posture, in order to assist his rising, caught hold of a shrub that grew near which, to his surprise, came easily out of the ground. On a closer examination he found that the earth had been recently disturbed. He therefore hailed his companions, and, with their assistance, re-opened the ground, where they found the body of our Master very indecently interred. They covered it again with all respect and reverence. and, to distinguish the spot, stuck a sprig of acacia at the head of the grave. They then hastened to Jerusalem to impart the afflicting intelligence to King Solomon, who, when the first emotions of his grief had subsided, ordered them to return and raise the body of our Master to such a sepulchre as became his rank and exalted talents; at the same time informing them that, by his untimely death, the Secrets of a Master Mason were lost. He therefore charged them to be particularly careful in observing whatever Casual Sign, Token, or Words might occur, whilst paying this last sad tribute of respect to departed merit. They performed their task with the utmost fidelity, for, on re-opening the ground, one of the Brethren looking round observed some of his

companions in this position we now know as the Sign of
Horror, being struck with the awfulness of the dreadful
and afflicting sight; while others, viewing the ghastly
wound still visible on the forehead of our Master, smote
their own thus in sympathy with his sufferings in a
posture we now know as the Sign of Sympathy. Two of
the Brethren then descended the grave, one of whom
endeavoured to raise the body by the Entered
Apprentice Grip, which proved a slip; the other then
tried the Fellowcraft Grip, which proved a slip likewise.
Having both failed in their attempts, a more zealous and
expert brother descended. and, using a word which
signified the builder is dead, raised him, with their
assistance, on the five points of fellowship: while
others, more animated, exclaimed a word meaning The
Builder is smitten, both Words having nearly a similar
import King Solomon therefore ordered that those
Casual Signs, Tokens, and Words should designate all
Master Masons throughout the universe, until time or
circumstances should restore the genuine ones. You will
have been given the words used during the ceremony of
your raising and I will not repeat them here.

It now only remains to account for the third Lodge of
Craftsmen. They had pursued their researches in the
direction of Joppa, and were meditating their return to
Jerusalem, when, passing the mouth of a cavern, they
heard sounds of deep lamentation and regret. On
entering the cave to ascertain the cause, they found three
men answering the description of those missing. who,
on being charged with the murder, and finding all
chance of escape cut off, made a full confession of their
guilt. They were then bound and led to Jerusalem.
where King Solomon sentenced them to that death
which the heinousness of their crime so justly merited,
executing them by having their bodies severed in two,

their bowels taken from thence and burned to ashes and the ashes scattered to the four winds of heaven, so that no trace or remembrance may be had of such vile and perjured wretches who had knowingly and willingly violated their solemn obligations as Masons.

Part 3

The Third-Degree Tracing Board

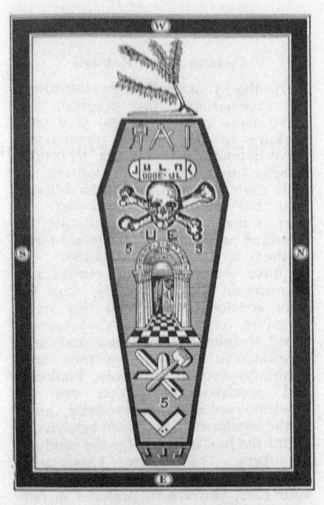

THE MASTER MASON

Reproduced by Kind Permission of Lewis Masonic

The Third-Degree Tracing Board

Our Master was ordered to be reinterred as near to the Sanctum Sanctorum as the Israelitish Law would permit – there in a grave, from the centre three feet East and three feet West, three feet between North and South, and five feet or more perpendicular.

He was not buried in the Sanctum Sanctorum itself, because nothing common or unclean was allowed to enter there, not even the High Priest but once a year, nor then until after many washings and purifications against the great day of expiation of sin, for, by the Israelitish law, all flesh was deemed unclean. The same fifteen trusty Fellowcrafts were ordered to attend the funeral of our Master, clothed in white aprons and gloves as emblems of innocence.

The ornaments of a Master Mason's Lodge are, the Porch, the Dormer, and the Square Pavement. The Porch was the entrance to the Sanctum Sanctorum: the Dormer, the window that gave light to the same; and the Square Pavement for the High Priest to walk on. The High Priest's office was to burn incense to the honour and glory of the Most High, and to pray fervently that the Almighty, of his unbounded wisdom and goodness, would be pleased to bestow peace and tranquillity on the Israelitish nation during the ensuing year.

The Tools with which our Master was slain were, as you have already been informed, the Plumb-rule, the Level, and the heavy Setting-maul. The Coffin, Skull, and Cross-bones are emblems of mortality, and allude to the untimely death of our Master, Hiram Abif, who was slain three thousand years after the creation of the world.

Along the top of his coffin were laid his Working Tools as a Master Mason, which are the Skirret, the Pencil, and the Compasses. The Skirret is an implement which acts on a centre pin. whence a line is drawn to mark out ground for the foundation of the intended structure; with the Pencil the skilful artist delineates the building on a draught or plan. for the instruction and guidance of the workmen; and the Compasses enable him with accuracy and precision to ascertain and determine the limits and proportions of its several parts. But as we are not all operative, but rather Free and Accepted, or Speculative Masons, we apply these Tools to our morals. In this sense, the Skirret points out to us that straight and undeviating line of conduct laid down for our pursuit in the Volume of the Sacred Law; the Pencil teaches us that our words and actions are observed and recorded by the Most High, to whom we must at last give an undisguised account of our conduct through life; and the Compasses remind us of His unerring and impartial justice, which, having defined for our instruction the limits Of good and evil, will either reward or punish us according as we have obeyed or disregarded His divine- commands.

Thus, the Working Tools of a Master Mason teach us to bear in mind, and act according to, the laws of our divine Creator, so that, when we shall be summoned from this sublunary abode, we may ascend to the Grand Lodge above, where the world's Great Architect lives and reigns forever.

Part 4

Using Your Working Tools to Build Your Soul

Using Your Working Tools to Build Your Soul

The most important thing to understand about Free-masonry is that its purpose is to facilitate your personal quest to build your character, and personality, and so develop your soul, (or as I, being a long-winded physicist, would call it, your divine inner spark of self-awareness that enables you to collapse Schrödinger wave functions and so create both a present reality and its past).

You are the sum total of your thoughts and actions. Freemasonry has traditionally used a symbolic word for this assemblage, and that word is Soul. It is a word that carries a lot of metaphysical baggage, but I think still works as a handy metaphor for the task that Free-masonry sets you, which is to encourage you to act and think in ways to improve yourself.

Bro Walter Leslie Wilmshurst summed this up when he said:

> You have an inside personality; a large psychological field usually called the Soul, which animates and actuates your outside self, but is far larger, more subtle, and complex than the latter. It bears the same relation to the outside self as the interior of the Lodge does to its exterior; and it is to the mysteries of your interior – your human soul – that the science of the Craft is entirely directed. The Lodge is formed as it is with the direct purpose of serving as a visible model of that sphere of psychical faculties and tendencies which we call the Soul, and to show how by the discipline of the Craft this inner part of each of us may be developed from a state of chaos to one of order and beauty, be wrought from the rough

ashlar to the perfect cube, and be transformed from its natural darkness into supranatural light.

Our Craft does this using the metaphor of building a temple, loosely based on the various historic structures which were built to house the Ark of the Covenant. But remember whenever Freemasonry uses the metaphor of a building it is talking about you, your personality, your intellect, your character, your soul.

The story of the Temple begins with the First, or Holy Lodge opened in the desert shade of the Tabernacle by Moses, Aholiab and Bazaleel, and goes down to the Third, or Grand and Royal Lodge opened by Zerubbabel, Haggai and Joshua, during the reconstruction of the Temple following the Babylonian captivity.

The focus of the three degrees of the Craft is on the Second, or Sacred Lodge opened by Solomon, king of Israel, Hiram, king of Tyre, and Hiram Abif, the widow's son, during the building of the First Temple on the threshing floor of Araunah. This being the site where Abraham had originally offered his son Isaac as a human sacrifice but had the offer rejected in favour of a ram.

The ritual of the three degrees of the craft, along with the additional workings of the board of Installed Masters, focuses on the methods and difficulties of constructing and consecrating this structure to the highest standards of building perfection. The Craft ritual makes use of Myth and Symbolism to assist a Master Mason to understand the problems of building his own character to the highest possible state of perfection he can attain.

To help in this task various tools are provided, and they are intended to be used to plan and implement the project to construct and consecrate your structure to the service of Brotherly Love, Relief and Truth.

Once you are raised to the sublime degree of a Master Mason you have access to all the working tools of a Craftsman, (although installed masters are given a further three to help in the management of the work-force, and Companions of the Holy Arch receive three additional inspirational tools). The nine Master Mason's tools arrive in three sets of three.

WORKING TOOLS OF AN ENTERED APPRENTICE

Speculative Masons apply these tools to their morals.

The 24-inch gauge

The 24-inch Gauge is to measure the operative's work.

In symbolic terms, the 24-inch gauge represents the twenty-four hours of the day, part to be spent in prayer to Almighty God, part in labour, refreshment, and sleep, and part in serving a Friend or Brother in time of need.

This spiritual tool is to help balance your daily time between three functions, each of equal value but not needing equal amounts of time. Its aim is to achieve a work/life balance. The three tasks are firstly, to attend to your spiritual tranquillity, to ensure you are at peace with yourself, with time to think and reflect. The second is to care for your person, and family. You must put the effort into your daily work to be able to look after yourself and your dependents. The third task is your altruistic obligation to those less happily placed. This is your work of charity. It should be done for the benefit of the recipient, not the glorification of the donor.

The Common Gavel

The common gavel is used for knocking all superfluous knobs and excrescences off your rough ashlar.

Symbolically, it represents the force of conscience and is used to subdue all vain and unbecoming thoughts, so that your words and actions ascend unpolluted to the throne of grace. The Master Mason learns that their body and soul, are the level ground upon which to build a cubical altar to symbolise their own spiritual life. No debasing habit of thought or conduct, should defile this work. Your apprentice's common gavel helps you to smooth the rough ashlar of your imperfect soul and fashion it into the perfect cubical altar that stands at the centre of your consciousness and symbolises your conscience. By using it skilfully you will learn to control anger and intolerance.

The Chisel

The chisel is used to smooth and prepare a stone for the hands of the more expert workman.

Symbolically, it calls attention to the advantages of an education, by which means alone we are rendered fit members of a regularly organized society. The chisel, when is driven by the force of conscience from the common gavel, chips away the rough exterior of a freshly quarried stone to uncover the perfect cube hidden within. Your education shapes your intellect, develops and expands your mind, broadens your perspective and makes you more civilized. The discipline of study and learning is a good habit to acquire, and Masons are all encouraged to make a daily step in Masonic knowledge.

WORKING TOOLS OF A FELLOWCRAFT

As before, Speculative Masons apply these tools to their morals.

The Plumb-rule

The Plumb Rule is used by the operatives to try, and to adjust uprights, whilst fixing them on their proper bases.

When moralised the ritual tells us that the infallible Plumb Rule, like Jacob's ladder, connects Heaven and Earth, and is your criterion of rectitude and truth. It instructs you how to walk justly and uprightly before God and man, turning neither to the right nor left from the path of virtue. As a builder raises his column by the level and perpendicular, so ought you conduct yourself to achieve due balance between avarice and profusion; to hold the scales of justice with equal poise; to make your passions and prejudices coincide with a just line for your conduct; and keep Eternity in view. The Plumb Rule teaches justness and uprightness of life and actions. With its close counterpart the plumb line, it denotes a silver cord which reaches from the mystical centre to link to your soul. This line forms a right angle to a level chord at the circumference. Here brethren wait in darkness for the rising of the bright morning star and the coming of the light of wisdom. As a Master Mason, you can use it to establish the direction of the centre, even if its mystery at first appears as darkness visible.

The Level

An Operative mason uses a level to lay down regular building sites and prove horizontals.

Symbolically the level symbolises that we all come from the same stock, partake of the same nature, and share the same hopes. Although distinctions of office are necessary to preserve authority, no eminence of situation should make us forget that we are Brethren. Even someone placed on the lowest rung of fortune's ladder is fully entitled to our regard. A time will come when all distinctions, save those of goodness and virtue, will cease, and Death, the great leveller will reduce us all to the same state. In this way the level teaches you equality. It is given to help you bring into balance and equality your senses, your emotions, and your intellect so that they play an equal part in assisting the interaction of your soul with the mystery of the centre. The level helps you model your consciousness in a way to subdue the peaks and troughs of your lower nature and bodily tendencies and help you detach your concerns from the changes of fortune and emotion to which you are subjected and enable you to regard the ups and downs of life as equal in educative value for you.

The Square

An Operative Mason uses their set square is to try, and adjust rectangular corners of buildings, and assist in bringing rude matter into due form.

It instructs us to regulate our lives and actions according to the Masonic line and rule, and to harmonize our conduct, to render us acceptable to that Divine Order from whom all goodness springs, and to whom we must give an account of all our actions. The Square brings rude matter into due form. It is by the Square that the business of Masonry may be managed with harmony and decorum. So, the Square teaches morality and how to control our actions. The Mason's square measures the accuracy of a right angle. Two squares make up an internal angle of a triangle and four squares describe the angle subsumed by the centre of a circle.

The Square is a perfect Platonic shape and can be assembled using sticks of three, four and five units. Your task, as a Mason, is to shape the roughhewn stone of your soul into a polished and perfect cube, being a three-dimensional representation of your perfected soul. This action is represented by four squares at the centre of a circle made up of your emotions, intellect, soul and spirit coming together in harmony to form a complete individual.

WORKING TOOLS OF A MASTER MASON

As before speculative Masons apply these tools to their morals.

The Pencil

With their pencil the skillful operative mason delineates the building in a draft or plan, for the instruction and guidance of the workforce.

Speculative masons apply this tool to their morals. In this sense your pencil teaches you that your words and actions are observed and recorded by the Almighty Architect, to whom you must give an account of your conduct throughout life. The wages of past bad behaviour are recorded upon your subconsciousness by the pencil that observes and there records all your thoughts, words and actions. You receive these wages without 'scruple or diffidence,' knowing yourself to be justly entitled to them and glad to purge yourself of old offences. You are always a debtor to someone or other for your present position in life and should repay what you owe to humanity. The pencil not only records your past it enables you to draw up the plans for a better future.

The Compasses

The compasses enable the operative mason to ascertain and determine the relative proportions and parts of their planned structure with accuracy and precision.

Symbolically the compasses keep you in due bounds with all mankind, particularly your Brethren in Free-masonry. The compasses belong in particular to every master mason, being the chief instrument you use for the organisation of architectural plans and designs. When united with the square, the compasses help you regulate your lives and actions as the compasses represent the functional energy of the spirit.

In the First Degree both points of the Compasses were hidden by the Square. In the Second Degree, one point was disclosed. In the Third both were exhibited. The implication was that as you progressed through the degrees, the inertia and negativity of your unreformed character became increasingly transmuted and superseded by the positive energy and activity of your Spirit. The upward-pointing Fire Triangle gradually assumed preponderance over the downward-pointing Water Triangle, signifying that as you develop as a Mason you become a more vividly living and spiritually conscious being.

The Skirret

The Skirret is an implement consisting of a cord which acts on a centre pin. The operative mason uses this cord to mark out the ground for the foundation of the intended structure.

Speculative masons apply this tool to their morals. In this sense, the Skirret represents a straight and undeviating line of conduct that is laid down for your pursuit in the Volume of the Sacred Law. The skirret symbolizes a tool to find the centre. When placed at the centre of a circle every point of the circumference is equidistance from its centre pin. Only by finding the centre can a Mason come to appreciate its mystery. Whilst reflecting on the role of Skirret you should reflect on how you can find the centre point of the circle of your being and so 'delineate the building' i.e. your soul, so that you can place the centre pin accurately and draw a true line to mark out the ground for the foundation of your intended structure.

These working tools are spread over Three Degrees of Mason knowledge. When you become a Master Mason these nine working tools are all you need to build your personal temple. The additional working tools of an Installed Master are management tools to assist in running a lodge and to plan its corporate work plan whilst the working tools of Royal Arch are to assist you to achieve inner mental well-being.

These Craft tools group into four main classes which spread are over the three degrees. These are:

- Tools of Physical Intervention
- Tools of Testing and Quality Assurance
- Tools of Planning and Measurement
- Tools of Thinking and Communication

The tools of physical intervention are the Common Gavel and the Chisel (They symbolise the force of your Conscience and the power of a liberal education)

The tools of testing and quality assurance are the Square, the Plumb Rule, the Level, and the Compasses. (They symbolise your sense of Morality, your sense of

Justice, your sense of Equality and your understanding of the boundary between good and evil)

The tools of planning and measurement are the 24-inch gauge and the Skirret. (They symbolize your ability to measure the materials needed for the construction, manage the time it will take to build the structure within a reasonable period and your ability to construct a perimeter which clearly defines your centre, that being the point where your divine spark of conscious awareness can be found.)

There is only one tool of thinking and communication, and that is the pencil. (This symbolises your ability to record, to plan, to organise your resources, and to communicate your plan to the workforce so that that they work together in harmony to complete the intended structure.)

Freemasonry gives you these tools to help you manage the project of building your own personality, character and soul. King Solomon's Temple is a metaphor for this work of soul-building. You are the building, and you create yourself using the mental tools which are analogies of the building tools our ancient brethren used to build King Solomon's Temple. The tools are not presented to you in the order in which you will need to use them to create an edifice of which you can be duly proud. But Freemasonry is not in the business of prescribing a course of action for you, instead it gives you a worthy objective, a model of good practice, a set of versatile tools and a group of companions to encourage you. It then tells you to think for yourself and get on with the job.

The tools are given to you in the context of three great lessons.

In the Entered Apprentice degree, you learn to face your fears and trust your lodge to guide you.

During the Fellowcraft degree, you develop your intellect by studying the hidden mysteries of nature and science to develop your understanding of the nature of Truth.

Then as a Master Mason you learn to face up to your own mortality and understand that your only real legacy is the knowledge and understanding you pass on. Your thoughts and deeds may live on, your body will not.

Freemasonry encourages you to think for yourself, it gives you objectives, models of good practice, a set of mental tools and a group of supportive companions to encourage you.

To help with this lifelong task it is useful to extend the fifteenth-century stone workers' metaphors to encompass modern thoughts on managing building projects, and in this section I have put down my ideas for applying this extended Masonic metaphor of soul-enrichment.

Let's begin by considering the steps needed to create this new structure that you hope to build, perfect in all its parts, and honourable to the builder.

UNDERSTAND THE PURPOSE OF YOUR BUILDING

First you must conceive the purpose of your building. When you joined Freemasonry, you were asked to name the predominant wish of your heart. You gave the ritual answer: light. This light is the faint glow of knowledge that you sense before you in the east and that you hope will develop from the faint ray of the bright morning star to the searing intensity of the noonday sun.

The purpose of your building is to be a structure fit to house all the complexity of your humanity—a space that can contain your emotions, your intellect, your spiritual aspirations, and that immortal essence of consciousness that makes you human and connects you to the Divine.

You are encouraged to build it on the sacred threshing ground of Masonic tradition which is considered holy for three ritual reasons.

The first is Abraham's ready compliance with the will of Great Architect in not refusing to offer up his son Isaac as a burnt sacrifice, before it pleased the Most High to substitute a more agreeable victim in his stead. (This symbolises your need to build your character upon a foundation of trust, to help you understand and learn about yourself.)

Second, the many pious prayers and ejaculations of King David, which stayed a pestilence then raging among his people, owing to his inadvertently having had them numbered. (This teaches that you must be prepared to acknowledge and make recompense for your previous mistakes, so you can start from a firm foundation.)

Third, the many thank offerings, oblations, burnt sacrifices, and costly donations that Solomon, King of Israel, made at the time of the completion, dedication, and consecration of the Temple at Jerusalem to the service of the Most High. (This shows that, if you persevere, you will eventually achieve the completion of your building, when you will be ready to open its dormer to the light of knowledge from the centre and to receive the accolade of your peers at its successful completion. This is signified in ritual myth, and musical allegory, as the arrival of the Queen of Sheba who hearing of the wonderful temple King Solomon had built was not content to simply send an ambassador to represent her but travelled in person with a great retinue to Jerusalem, to view the glories of the building and offer to Solomon many costly gifts to adorn it.)

Having determined that your building will stand on Holy ground you must next define the extent of your own holy ground. (Mine is firmly founded in a deep-seated belief in the Laws of Physics and the importance of consciousness in creating and giving purpose to the great scheme of the cosmos). Next you must survey your site to align it along the line of the first rays of the rising sun on the summer solstice, the moment when light triumphs over darkness. You will need to mark the line of shadow of the deacon's wand on the pre-prepared ground to align your foundation stone at the northeast corner of the cleared site.

Symbolically the form of your temple will need to be a parallelepiped. In length from East to West, in breadth between North and South, in depth from the surface of the earth to the centre, and as high as the Heavens. (This symbolises the universal extent of the Masonic know-ledge you intend to house within the finished temple of yourself.)

The tools required for creating this objective are your pencil, your mind and your awareness of Truth. Your awareness of the existence of truth inspires you, your mind translates this awareness into your actions and your pencil outlines the steps you need to take to prepare a plan to complete a temple dedicated to the three great principles of Brotherly Love, Relief and Truth.

OUTLINE THE STRUCTURE, COMPONENTS, SITE, AND DRAW UP A PLAN

The major Tools you will use are the 24-inch gauge, the Skirret and the Pencil. In this step you must outline the structure, its components and its site, to draw up a plan.

At the Centre of your building, you will need to make space to house a special symbol in the roof of its middle chamber. This is the letter G situated in the Centre of a blazing star, and it denotes the divine spark of your conscious intelligence whose self-awareness makes you part of the purpose of the universe.

You can plan the extent of the middle chamber using the skirret, and, by noting the position of the centre pin you can mark the site where the divine spark will reside, once you have completed a building fit to house it.

The scope and extent of the stories of the building, the layout of the spiral stairway and shape and size of the necessary component ashlars must all be added to your plan using the pencil, which records and communicates ideas, and the skirret, which plots circumferences and spirals, in conjunction with the 24-inch gauge, which measures the dimensions of the stones that must be shaped in the quarry before being assembled on the building site in accordance with the plan you have prepared.

PLAN YOUR TIME TO TAKE ADVANTAGE OF QUARRY DEW

It is important that the stones are squared, dressed or otherwise shaped, soon after they are extracted from the quarry whilst the stone is fresh from the earth and suffused with the quarry sap that makes it easy to work. Once shaped, the stones must be seasoned by exposing them to the open air to dry the quarry sap and harden their form.

Once shaped and seasoned, the stones will become hardened and difficult to work, so whilst making your plan you must take account of the need to establish a steady rate of progress, using the time-measure aspect of the 24-inch gauge. You should learn from the practice of our ancient brethren under the guidance of Hiram Abif, who decreed that the stones should be hewn in the quarry, there squared, carved, marked, and numbered according to the plan, whilst still fresh. After due seasoning they should be conveyed to Jerusalem and set in place with wooden mauls and implements prepared for that purpose. You should emulate the excellence of the Craft in those days, so that your materials, even though they might be prepared at a great distance in other parts of your life, when they are brought to your temple should come together so that each piece fits with exact nicety. In that way your design appears more like the work of the Great Architect of the Universe than that of human hands.

The 24-inch gauge, which symbolises the twenty-four hours of the day, reminds us that all necessary work must be done at the correct time. The shaping and dressing must not be delayed, the seasoning must not be rushed, and the numbered ashlars must be shipped to the building site in the order they are needed to fulfil your plan. You have little spare storage space so the component parts must arrive just in time, neither too late (so delaying the work), nor out of sequence (so requiring a search for the missing parts), nor yet too quickly (thus cluttering up the building site and making the work more difficult).

ASSEMBLE YOUR WORK FORCE AND YOUR RAW MATERIALS

The major tool you will use is the Pencil. In this step you must note down the workforce and the raw materials you need. As a Master Mason you will already have been introduced to the four components of your being that constitute your work force.

Your First-Degree Work Force. In the first degree you faced your emotions, which imbued you with fears and hopes. You learned to control and subdue your fears and improper urges to focus your hopes and inspiration on your search for Truth.

Your Second-Degree Work Force. In the second degree you developed your mind and intellect. You studied the hidden mysteries of nature and science that you might better understand the mystery of being and learn to face and recognise Truth. You were taught the need to climb the spiral stairway towards the Centre, even though the spiral path was concealing your ultimate destination.

Your Third-Degree Work Force. In the third degree you learned how to free your spirit from the tyranny of your ego and let it spiral towards the light of the sacred symbol at your centre, even though it was still hidden from your view.

Now you need to recruit an overseer. As you muster your resources to labour both in the quarry and on the building site, you must also harness the insight of your soul, which recognises its oneness with the divine spark that motivates the implementation of your plan. You are now ready to mine the quarries.

Having listed with your pencil the disposition of your workforce you must next think about which quarries they can mine for the rough ashlars of your building. These quarries are traditionally known as the seven liberal arts and sciences which are: **Grammar, Rhetoric, Logic, Arithmetic, Geometry, Music and Astronomy.** Each of the liberal arts offers different types of stone for the various chambers of your building. Freemasonry encourages you to mine these quarries of rough nuggets you extract to shape the smooth ashlars your plan requires.

Once again, your pencil comes to your aid, helping you to organise your thoughts and take notes about your growing knowledge of yourself as you learn to speak clearly and with feeling, express your thoughts logically, account for your actions, appreciate the eternal truths of geometry, imbibe the sweet joy of music and appreciate the beautiful majesty of the heavens.

CREATE THE COMPONENTS AND CHECK THEIR FIT

For this step your major Tools are the Common Gavel, the Chisel, the Square, and the Compasses. The purpose of this step in the process is to create the component parts of your personal temple and check that they meet the requirements of your plan. The method of squaring and shaping a rough ashlar is painstakingly slow. You need to learn caution, remember to measure, and check before you use the hammer. Once the chisel bites into the stone it is changed forever. You must trust the plan and constantly refer your evolving work to the blueprint, to check your components are correctly shaped.

The key to success at this stage is developing your craftsmanship, taking pride in your work and appreciating that each stone in the plan, no matter how small, or how apparently oddly shaped, is needed and vital to complete the structure. It means working to deadlines, delivering high quality finished stones on time, and systematically selecting the best available raw material.

You must first sharpen your chisel. The importance of using the chisel at this stage cannot be overemphasised. Stones are not shaped by emotion or good intentions. Without the sharp cutting edge of a highly honed education, you cannot hope to cut the stone cleanly and beautifully. If you think the cost of training and education is too expensive to consider, then reflect for a moment on the immense cost and consequences of ignorance. It is better to apply skill and knowledge in small cutting steps, than to wreck the stone by ill-considered random blows which crack and destroy it.

ORGANISE THE PROCESS AND QUALITY OF CONSTRUCTION

The major tools you will use are the Common Gavel, the Plumb Rule, the Level and the Compasses. The purpose of this step is to organize the construction process and check the quality of construction. You must appoint trusted overseers, drawn from your internal workforce, to second check your efforts and reject any stones which are not up to standard or which do not fit the plan.

Now you must implement the construction process. Your plan relies on a correctly shaped stone arriving at the building site at the exact moment it is needed to further the construction of the building, so that you can use a Master's trowel to set it in place using the mortar of Brotherly Love. As you build, you will start by checking the levelness of the site, you will align the corner stone using the light of the rising sun on the day of greatest light. As you set each stone in place you will check its alignment with the level and the plumb rule, adjust it, if necessary, with gentle taps from the gavel of conscience and measure its relative position to its fellows using the compasses to check you are doing what is right. As the building progress you will require a plumb line of Moral Rectitude and Truth to make sure your walls are upright and worthy.

Now you need to quality check your construction work. When the building is complete, you are ready to dedicate it by calling down the glory of the Shekinah into the middle chamber, ensuring that the light of knowledge can permanently dwell at your centre.

Before we leave this topic, it might be useful to consider the progressive nature of Freemasonry's ritual. You begin by having Freemasonry done to you. During this process you are given the tools and shown the nature of the intended structure. Freemasonry is done to you. Next you do Freemasonry to others, and, as you progress through the offices of the lodge, you learn more about the construction process, and the use of the tools, and you get hints about the nature of the overall plan.

This knowledge is consolidated when you take on the office of Master of the Lodge, where you become the overseer. Then you are given work force management tools and taught how to quality assure your final structure. You are trained, by holding office, to present yourself as a just, upright and impartial role model. Your task is to prepare your completed temple to be humbly consecrated by the light of Truth and Brotherly Love.

Only when all these steps have been completed is your building ready to be consecrated to its original purpose and you are finally ready to take up the contemplative and supportive office of IPM where you can reflect on what you have learned and begin to inhabit the soul-structure you have created for yourself.

Brethren I wish you well with the Management of your Individual Soul-Building Projects.

[]

Using the Masonic Tutor Support Website

The Masonic Tutor Support Website is open to all
Master Masons and is hosted by
http://www.Openlodge.com.
It is accessed via The Web of Hiram website.
The Web of Hiram was created by Robert whilst he
was a lecturer at Bradford University's School of
Management. He decided to create an electronic
database of the Masonic material held in many of the
University's Special Collections as part of his on-going
research into the cultural origin of scientific ideas.
For further details go
http://www.webofhiram.org
From the home page of The Web of Hiram click on
the Masonic Tutoring link and select the link to Vol 4.

Other books by Robert Lomas:

The Masonic Tutor's Handbooks:
   Vol. 1: *The Duties of the Apprentice Master*
   Vol. 2: *Freemasonry After Covid 19*
   Vol. 3: *Becoming a Craftsman*

W.L. Wilmshurst's The Ceremony of Initiation *Revisited*
W.L. Wilmshurst's The Ceremony of Passing *Revisited*

Turning the Hiram Key
Turning the Templar Key
Turning the Solomon Key

Freemasonry and the Birth of Modern Science
Freemasonry for Beginners
The Invisible College
The Lewis Guide to Masonic Symbols
The Lost Key
A Miscellany of Masonic Essays
The Secret Power of Masonic Symbols
The Secret Science of Masonic Initiation
The Secrets of Freemasonry
The Templar Genesis of Freemasonry

The Man Who Invented the Twentieth Century
Mastering Your Business Dissertation
The Pant Glas Children

Translated from the Welsh of Daniel Owen:

Rhys Lewis
Ten Nights in the Black Lion
The Seven Sermons of Daniel Owen
Methodist Characters of Mold

Co-authored with Chris Knight

The Book of Hiram
The Hiram Key
The Second Messiah
Uriel's Machine

Co-authored with Geoff Lancaster

Forecasting for Sales and Materials Management

Kindle eBooks by Robert Lomas:

W.L. Wilmshurst's The Ceremony of Initiation *Revisited*
W.L. Wilmshurst's The Ceremony of Passing *Revisited*

Turning the Hiram Key
Turning the Solomon Key
Turning the Templar Key Part 1 – The True Origins of Freemasonry

Freemasonry and the Birth of Modern Science
The Invisible College
The Lost Key
A Miscellany of Masonic Essays
The Secret Science of Masonic Initiation
The Secrets of Freemasonry
The Templar Genesis of Freemasonry

The Man Who Invented the Twentieth Century
Mastering Your Business Dissertation
The Pant Glas Children

Rhys Lewis *by Daniel Owen. A New Translation from the Welsh*

Printed in Great Britain
by Amazon